Manic Rose City

Lucas Klesch

Words of Praise for Manic Rose City:

The Danger

“With cool phrases like ‘Brutal Blues’ and ‘Leaves of Industry,’ Manic Rose City evokes imagery like Bob Dylan’s in Blonde on Blonde.”

“I love the abstract phrasing, disco lemonade, vigilante art, etc. Those are the kinds of phrases that really kick a reader in the nuts, makes ‘em think a little in different ways, and opens up ideas and possibilities.”

Juan Valdez

“The work, I see and read as lyrics to songs like Steely Dan’s hopped up on a Jazzy Rock style!”

This book is for Pauline Kawecki, my beatnik grandma who introduced me to Dylan Thomas, Emily Dickinson, and having coffee in a coffee shop!

And for all the lads, Rose City till I die...

 Portland

manic rose city poetry & prose

low reflection
quite simply
Rose City Blues # 2
Mania Blues # 1
Rose City Blues # 10
Mixed Energy
Burnside Bridge
Unified Theory
No-thing
Visceral Experience
Verbose Zen
Zoom!
311 News
Mania Junkie
El Fresco Klesch
light switch physiology
US Blues
deconstructing l + j + k
untitled # 2
kat call
Ashbury Dreams
Laurel thirst's First Fridays
Rose City Blues # 13
say hey!
ex-pat news
Rose City Blues # 3
59 cents
underworld
Audible Reality
Brugh Azul
untitled muse
Rose City Blues # 8
Mania Blues # 2
Azure's Words
ljk's muse
daft hands

Jive Cup
walking with royalty
303 NW Park
pole to pole
Rose City Blues # 4
Yamhill Pub Rant
Songs from 107

Ode to frësch Klesch

ode to frësch klesch as a memory
not so lost in chaotic energy.
ladders back to confident thoughts again
it started with a kiss
sex so wonderful humane perfection
time dictates movements in a post-911 world

ode to frësch klesch as a love note.
a reminder to rise each morning
give myself a hug - i sleep to wake again
landscape of chaotic energy
State structured emotional boundaries
positive vibrations for the negative fear
the way to ruin walk it again
no more i am frësch

ode to frësch klesch as a gospel serenade.
i am transparent cascading emotional chaos
comfort resides in tolerance
tiny gifts, little messages, a touch, a smile, a wink
hugs give joy and anticipation of future care
kisses ignite fire - flames express love
between warm sheets like silk and Zen

ode to frësch klesch a declaration
no waiting in vain
i know wonderful now
imagine fine wine
aged for perfection
as frësch klesch's design

Halloween 2003

at once a crisp break
like a light switch
so easily on or off
the decent rappel
with lunatic filters
cascading emotional crisis
changing faces spiral away
then flat i lay
realizing the falsity of filters

at once light switch illumination
madness lost to reality
rose instead of black-
one deep breath
and i am at it again

at once knowingly aware
this useless energy
a compendium of chemical thoughts
i only follow to conclusion
spent and beleaguered by this emotional destruction

at once lucky if i can sleep
light switch insomnia compels more crisis in energy-
and the dichotomy of this landscape
lucky when i sleep to wake again

Back Bay, Boston

in this motion a loss
released   punk drunk
like the night with Bukowski
in the Back Bay, Boston
it was spring, but bitter
a few derelicts and street walkers
softly the night fades
continual release
tantric love   punk drunk
springing as the sun rises
we finish in a tussle of rumpled pillows
matted hair
in a motion   lost
    spoonin'   in the Back Bay

Six Directions

iconoclastic – grandiose
something otherworldly tainted our lives
never quite fully whole
pay homage to the six sacred directions
two polar halves, opposite, conflicting
perched for a discreet moment
    not a fit - wanderlust
always learning ever-changing chaos
shifts in energy
usable and wasteful
move, move, move

Rose City Blues # 5

four jack and cokes, two jays
just to lay head to rest
wanderlust manic rose city
how i travel her streets
altered and observant
i see you watching me
at the Annex on Thursdays
in the Low Brow Lounge
we always smile knowing
fate is twisted false
i seek it always close
me – i see me – changing
i cannot find it - you
twisted is my mind
sought by energy
consuming all normalcy
I can only wander watching

Rose City Blues # 7

its not quite one pm
   three beers   two jays
and I cannot explain how the shabbos comes
sacred is the day
     a holy morning of lovin‘
me at a dive bar after sundown
    full of drunken lunacy
harlots and joes playin‘ desire
     I am here drinkin‘ and smoking
watching a disturbed world
          from the fisheye
                  through the glass
     fogged must be the brain
          erased by a solvent
cigarettes for hussies and harlots

Euro Slut

so long in you i swim
awash with desire
speaking every measure
once true design
i kissed your sultry lips
revel in the taste
of warm cinnamon on rustic fall days
as red + gold line the path to your heart
i see you smiling sultry
with your lit fag
remember London
fog and warm beer
we saturated the city
our foreplay a public display
in alleys, at bars
drunk in the tube
kissing laughing
at once in Paris, Venice, Nice'
lovin' each other
we saw the show
red light dancing
salty sweet kisses
musty scents
sex in the city
on the stairs in each park
our desire for each other
unmasked exploration in the flat

opium den dreams smoky sex
mystical skin our wet bodies sapped
lethargy - two weeks, five months
i swim in you erotic saturation
never taming our sultry kisses
time lost time spent
naked and asleep
bodies on fire
awash with desire

Late Night at the Annex

feverishly, move, move, move
    late night at the Annex
        she smiles, i drink
cigarettes streaming
    late night at the Annex
feverously, smile, smile, smile
  a curve in her lips
        and i take another drag
   smoke and smiles
another late night at the Annex
outside, on the streets
        drunks and derelicts
        cops and bums
    late night at the Annex

Rose City Blues # 27

midnight,   manic rose city
   the strange and surreal
      kinky night   sultry
    jazz   tea dreams
wakeful   energy   cracks
as i pound the streets
  walking,   talking gibberish
              broken accents

two a.m., oh rose city
     drunken frenzies
  brutal blues   -   cops on the beat
  melee on the street
     no courage beyond observing
     the proverbial drunken jock fight
  non-linear affairs
                 strange life cycles
 the aware human walks
    different faces self-defining
  manic streams
                   in my mind

NOW!

now, long since i looked upon that golden field
hay streams washed gold by the sun,
my pictures of you strewn along glittering horizons
as we once shared the morning space
quiet and nestled – our skin saturated as lovers.

now, long since i remember seeing you the first time-
a story spoken as a bard would claim any modern
renaissance - only dark and quintessential as a
silhouette of vine along the rusted path – leaves of
industry.

now, forgotten beyond which i see no more dreams
– no memories in a childlike haze chasing butterflies
down the street in summer sun with dirty bare feet
we played tag while holding hands.

now, i feel your energy – skin, breath
tantalizingly fresh along our endings
so far in heaven – a divine humbleness and praise
back of a cab, martini's high with soft touches small
kisses
we swim in cold creeks – down a ravine in Fall
warm red we strip
Autumn leads to Winter and rebirth
like each night i sleep to wake again.

now, nothing more remembered by smell alone-
yet faint vanilla responds,
slanting kisses down soft pale skin
a neck like lavender fields.

now, it reminds me of sunny mornings
in that Paris room waking always at 10 a.m.
sun warming white sheets interlaced bodies in a
tussle left after love.

now, in a rain soaked day
dark clouds lead to clean skies
pale blue breaks like soft patches of skin
trailing your lower back.

now, i miss the comfort of vanilla dreaming skirts
at the Annex drinking whiskey
in the cellar bar with laughter
a smile, like kids and ice cream.

now, a blue bike on the corner
late evening breeze supple like a nipple before arousal
one bar after another i go
till i walk cobbled streets wet by rain.

now, beyond the similarity a smell-
a taste, sensual existence in both memory & reality
continual, perpetual – as the sun rises
always mourning white sheets vanilla

untitled

a single strand of dark black hair
    lie on square tile
    centered on shower wall
    remnants and reminders
happy are all the days she occupies his waking thoughts
    once a figment
        first a nymph
                sometimes a wraith
        always his paramour
in life magic, in love mystery
    exploration is best in abandon
    abandon only when self-aware

Rose City Blues # 9

crisp night almost November
no rain in the rose city
two a.m., on the Burnside Bridge
my pace forlorn
thoughts drifting to memories
with the promise of warmth you bring
late night alone
walking home
sleep to wake tomorrow cold
your lovely tender kisses i miss
flowing golden dreams
heart marrow sparkles
sensual as it drips from my fingers
our warm skin careening kisses
the north park blocks, two a.m.
rustle of the Fall leaves
i kick in cadence
us laughing like kids
on wet nights
in this manic city
blues stretched thin
i sleep to wake again

Free Sex No Love

American Spirit cigarettes
blended Irish whiskey the ritual,
smoke a jay
take a shot
drag on a Spirit
Jameson kisses
with a New York hippie chick
free sex no love
screaming the rapture
she loves a dry tonic
no more the spiritual than a love of sex
detached like the cap of our empty whiskey bottle
one more toke and the clothes are strewn
free sex no love
three a.m. cries in rapture
drag on a spirit, sweet sleep surrenders
walking Hawthorne at noon
no modern Haight Ashbury - just
free sex no love

Rose City Blues # 12

an evening in a manic rose city
    the energy and vibe wanders
not a matter of the heart
    more drink and tea
  hepcats at the Annex
         drink chasing ideas
my body longs for you
    yet the city sent us away
         me, lucid with probity
         you, sexy and looking
in my induced way – i miss those soft lips
   like quiet rain for the rose city
    ripe in Portland proper
   freshly historic   organic
i confess, i love this manic city – a mirror image,
my home   sensual reminders   us
    vanilla skin   matted wet
   the cycle   rise and fall
move in close   farther away
      dichotomy of the city
            metaphoric people mimic
a manic rose city

Balloons on Parade

if i wasn't me
then who could i be?
just a new variation of the old
a plumber, a bartender, a man
a woman, someone of consequence
i am all you make of me
and all i despise
i hope i understand
what compassion shows
once a man beloved truth
kind justice
so lost in chasing the divine
i am me, now,
i am here, waiting –
for a parade of plumbers, bartenders, and crooks
heroes' to my generation of lost souls
waiting to grow old to be someone

the blue light

what design?
no rest for weary hearts
who walk the sands of concrete fields
in asphalt parks where kids play
with glass pipes, spent needles, savage dreams
born to a post 9-11 world
imperial and subversive
"with us or against us"
dissent is terrorism
freedom a forgotten democracy
democracy a veiled dictatorship
oppressive in the repressive few   power resides
a populace, fear perpetual mind killers
the blue light sucked dry
a populace, prone in malice
subliminal desert oasis of false images
what design?

Drunken Lunacy

no, say -   me, boy
so, her   night stream
    be a boy, a girl
          nude   sex   yes,
  say me,   go   yes
  no,   move move move
silent crush weight dry
  she laughs then wakes, stolen cream
be cream and strange red hysteria
    long black pubic hairs
golden floor   hard and cold
  we mingle   chaos   so,
  heads, tongues, signs, so tactile
i want to fuck – fornicate in primal chaos
        express this useless energy for positive
i am beyond the endless stream of bizarre statistics
     and red face flush stolen cream

East Coast Romance

i stand, wait,   you
walk   go   stand
on the corner we kiss
smile like school children
red blush
lips wet desire
fingers like velvet
we stroll worn cobbles
of histories romance
petals bloom
on streets filled by onlookers
in the commons
on the park bench
Boston in spring
love blooms
i   you   stroll on cobbles
in Beacon Hill   fingers
worn   entwined
like vines on the Brownstone
in histories wake
steal a kiss
amongst Boston's masses
faces smile
on histories romance

us, soft eyes
a kiss
on the corner
in the park
warm cobbles
standing divine
we laugh like kids
plush lips red in spring
sweet rhythm design
fresh with joy
playing with the divine

Rose City Blues # 11

funk and the bop
hepcats dressed tight
smoky bar   crowded floor
jumpin' with a honey tonight
tonic screams   smoke dreams
dancing with your baby tonight
Black Angel   soul and funk
no west-L.A. fade away
this is the Rose City
a dichotomy of the dream
sustainable grassroots
posh socialites
a green rose city
manic nights
wet dark days
liquid sunshine
for a lucid drunken haze
funk and the bop
late night hepcats
dancing the ladies   tonic screams
a dichotomy of the dream
for a manic Rose City

Saturation skin to skin

no, today belongs not to me
but a useless energy, restless
wet sidewalks   dreary clouds
with grayscale skies
you, i saw you smile
warm   like a red wine
euphoric   drunk
bare skin   touch
me, a sensual endeavor saturated with desire
play for the self-aware
a dream unrealized
skin to skin
we, commingle   in the dark
latent excitation
two brazen dreams fulfilled
no, today belongs to saturation
energy useless to me
a sensual endeavor
just to stay sane
intoxication to sleep
sleep to wake again

Wanton Muse

three hours and i left you to him,
three hours of sleep i stole away
i wanted to stay
your vibrant energy flowing sensual
a sparkle upon every fiber
i trembled with joy
a soft voice in the darkness
reach out and touch me
i feel you everywhere,
your warmth and joy like a
healing blanket laid upon my wounds
you, my muse
a delicate flower   so bold
with your twisted spirit
i know you seek praise,
and a calm pool to cleanse
so confident yet undefined
time spent priming a pump
three hours of sensual play
on the corner of your bed
on the floor – i leave you primed for him,
three hours, and i am in the back of a cab
urban smoke   my muse   its 3 a.m.
i feel you like pin pricks along my skin
three hours of sleep
and i still feel your   sensuality

Rose City Blues #1

rain sapped streets
        i walk on Sundays
     restless but filled
  i walk   for coffee,
                  watching,
   to ease my mind
puddles in concrete
   Sundays are empty
              i walk
     restless but filled
fields of concrete cobblestone
like roads that do not lead to Rome
rain for a sunny day
        in the rose city

A World in Circus

like Bronco, a slender tall man from Croatia
my soul is burdened by the atrocities of this world
the chaos of the city a small soothing balm
we definitely live an estranged existence
not quite a prophet like Nesta
more a witness of the stories
the chaos of the city echoes the State function
of my Soul - troubled by Bronco's truths
a mirror to the world i know
no sanctity and no rest - watch, experience
like a balm one cannot find satisfaction in
Sartre experienced it, existential strife –
a realization you are here, now what?
i am troubled by my generation's blinders
not quite frozen, but drawn
to the indistinguishable mess
always is the outcome –
like nesta and the cornerstone
hiding, i see them all – leaving faint glimpses
always passing in time, my generation
lost in indistinguishable chaos and carnival mirrors

Rose City Blues # 6

is it early -   is it late?
    woke to a summer sun
bombastic and a little outrageous
    frësch klesch on the street
  Carlsberg in Red
                blue shaded eyes
        frësch in every way
  the style and class of comfort
home Red bright in the sun
Liverpool f.c.,   outrageous
    tossers and scousers
  from the north country
        industrial dark towers
  working class hooligans
it is early   from a late night
  rebel rousing with the lads
        carousing   drink
in a daft rose city

Soul Food

soul food
in conversation
soul food
in music
soul food
in art
soul food
in you
grab paw
kiss yes
more! more!
grab paw
smile kiss
more!
more!
you cry
soul food is life

Rose City Mornings

Mornings without the sun after
crazy night wanderings
tea dreams in waking
a cup of café'
to delight a hepcats awakening mind

Mornings without the sun after
nights sold to pleasure
kat's met at Jimmy Mak's
tuning some jazz tea
drinks and the lads jumpin'

Mornings without the sun after
long waking nights   wanderlust
warm somber mumblings
tea and the beloved café'
no kat's to quench the thirst

Mornings without the sun
lead to blue sky afternoons
street walking with camera
mind chasing words expressive
many smiles   ecstatic

Mornings without the sun
lead to rainy afternoons
spent exploring tactile relations
intermingled design for sustenance
languishing red kisses

Mornings without the sun
lead to evenings in comfortable arms
barfly's and artists
on the cool walk down Burnside
cops chasing bums
derelicts chasing drink
gay boys, Stark street queers
hepcats stroll tea dream whistles

Stark Street Scene

Trumpets roaring a bebop tune
    candlelight dances
                        upstairs at the Annex
smiling Sax,   foot tapping
    hepcat entertaining the ladies
drinkin‘ and puffin leaf

Stark street books
    second floor squares
        glass balcony affairs
    from street level scenes

Stark street queers
    boys, rag tag tag
          miles beyond blue
like the beatniks chasing cultured jazz
   in transcendental tea dreams
words spun in the village
    like my disenchanted intellectual friends
        more bored   lost

Stark street   Rose City
     rag tag tag
    candlelight dances
                        upstairs at the Annex

Stark street   Rose City
pimps and queers
    punk street kids   cops
        more bored than lost

Stark street beggars   realize
      no chains of bondage
         this generation is free
hepcat with the ladies
      second floor laughter

Stark street scenes
   a new lover from the street below
  drunken boy kisses
      a wet delight to watch

jay jay first '04

mirthful earth in its flaccid cadence
        its snowing
        its snowing
    azure is snowing
            bright energy beam everywhere
    azure is sound
            light energy cascading scream
    azure is everyone
        its snowing
        its snowing
            on the first day of ought four
mirthful earth in its flaccid cadence
  footfalls on corn starch
      sound muffled by thick white air
  foot patterns moving everywhere
      pristine sound cascade
    azure is snowing
            zen words of positive joy
mirthful earth in its flaccid cadence

Beautiful Rose City # 5

an evening turns to night
    beautiful manic rose city
erotic passion   fire
    repeating hands
          on baby blue silk
    erotic fingers   kneading
    sensual pressure   chakras
energy pulsing   warm core
    soft moans as hands massage
  erotic energy   -   feet, calves, thighs
        hand energy flowing
    sweet taste on my lips
    moans in pleasure as climax after climax
pulses vibrant energy
        hands kneading blue
    passion kisses   wet

sweet taste of you
  on red plush lips we kiss
    all night our bodies mingle
    sleep only moments as heat prods
bodies   flush with desire   saturation
        the heat of intercourse
    insatiable fluid motion
        intimate orgasm - potent
  energy pulsing screams
      release together
our bodies relax   sleep   seven a.m.

Oh beautiful rose city
passionate skin touches
our bodies warm Joy
snuggled naked sleep
a perfect shabbos of love
we wake to sun in december
smiles on saturated skin
sensual energy for a beautiful rose city

Nine A.M. Soul

rose city, nine a.m.
  our bodies warm against each other
    soft skin like petals
        floating on vanilla sea
    each morning and time the same sun
warms us like Paris
          and the gold delight of café'

rose city, nine a.m.
  i can feel your breath
    so light in your dreams
        soft skin   placed lips
a light kiss on the back
  blue eyes smile at me
     as the sun warms us

rose city, ten a.m.
  our shabbos spent in each other
     discovering golden heart marrow
        liquid sparkling hands
  we stroll tertiary streets
    glowing smile   arm in arm
        fresh sun warms faces
    our day of play   admiring
each comfort of mornings
         skin to skin

rose city, one p.m.
  not quite punk drunk in love
    the park our play date
        on the swings
                    in the grass
   we kiss as lovers
      laugh like children

rose city, nine am
  i wake to your warm skin
    soft kisses start the day
        a slice of the divine pale blue
nine a.m. soul for the rose city

shards, shadows and porcelain

          stars and shadows
     soft plush tan
the light green ink on her supple skin
     flows like velvet from a faucet
     beset by diamonds
          stars and shadows
   on her arm   the
lone star on arched back
     dark eyes   swimmingly grand
         express delicate beauty
   refined childish innocence
         before the madness prevails
darkness brings shadows
     bodies skin to skin
          shreds of light
                    sparkle and writhe
like diamonds on plush skin
          stars and shadows
     celestial screams
soft sighs in a tangle of titan bliss
     shimmering glare
          moistened skin on skin
muffled gestures a supple response
   hands crave a porcelain balm
     apply the glaze
          stars or shadows
   all brilliant luminosity

Untitled # 1

i could see you
could you see me?
i looked up and you were gone
i missed you then as i miss the blonde
vanilla skirts we wore in bed together
i could see you
could you see me? do you miss me?
why say "i love you" after you leave
what a cunning ruse bisexuality is
convenient justification of fear-self-loathing
i am not your history of pain
i am not your pattern of control
you cannot say "i love you" after you leave
there is no meaning in the i
just as time dictates i will forget to miss you
can you feel me? do you remember the blonde vanilla
skirts we wore?
i still feel you – sometimes on Saturday
when the sun shines – or was that you're Saturday –
Tuesday at three a.m.
after arousal spent on painted skin
i can see you
can you see me? do you miss me?
i cannot say 'i love you' after you leave
the words have no meaning i can express

untitled shite for bill

bill bell read a poem about me
for days i toiled to remember his words –
        a fear heard echoed in my lovers' touches
                felt in their eyes
they think i walk with Bukowski, Thomas and Hemingway
        to die before some preordained time –
                with posthumous volumes left behind
ah, – one thing to reflect
    i surpassed the rock star curse of twenty-seven
        thirty Christ-like years i see beyond
  yet death is a release
                from this organized life
a gift of energy to an entropic universe

blue ribbon insomnia

awake at one a.m.
    energized skin post-play
        city glow on dark dry skies
awake at two a.m.
    not quite asleep yet
        eyes closed by physical action
awake at three a.m.
    the night sky often dark
        spent by pleasure
awake at four a.m.
    lying on my back
        eyes glazed outside
awake at five a.m.
    a blue ethereal glow
        permeates outlined windows
awake at six a.m.
    light golden glowing clouds
        strewn within pale sky
awake at seven a.m.
    blue sky sunrise
        daydreaming window eyes
awake at eight a.m.
    face to the high yellow moon
        a golden start to play

low reflection

here i sit
a bitter drunk
more melancholy
than drunken lunacy
is this mud on my shoes
or is it sand from the walk
a choice so existential i live
testing life as many theories
dynamic love the equation
boy + girl two variables
chance, luck, circumstance...
a choice to trust – mere simplicity
why sleep tonight?
i am neither verbose nor gregarious
more triumphantly melancholy
a dichotomy of choice – divergent theories
night again i sit a low reflection

quite simply

simply often, i walk to stroll
        excess energy   instability
    if spoken in haste
        long after blue eyes turn gray
simply often, i see blue –
        greens and a dirty brown
    mourning black skirts
                laid bare by design
simply often, i am self-aware
        swimming between white seas
    seeing in a morning sun
                velvet skin dyed blue
simply often, i wait anxiously
        watch a smile clear
    parsed pale skin seas
                spoken energy a stroll

Rose City Blues # 2

life mingles at man-made intersections
   in golden sunshine on concrete corridors
inane weapons of mass-destruction
continually rolling by
        a fashion show parade
of posh socialites
ever-changing hair color whores,
the bourgeoisie hipsters, and drunk punk sluts
        crisply careening vacant strides
oh no honey!
        if you cannot walk in your shoes
elegance – grace – style
        if you cannot walk in your shoes
oh no honey!   you are not sexy
        if you cannot walk in your clothes
grace – elegance – style
    few carry style with pizzazz
                or charisma to command attention
        sexuality sells this passing parade
    the few as role-models
        most are fodder for the sheep

Mania Blues # 1

cascading emotional landscape
    snapped clean by tragedy
        awake to be aware
lost emblem of the divine
    stolen by my last lover
        awake in the Tullie fog
walking the Golden Gate
    at three a.m. on Thursdays
i remember Boston in spring
    strolling the St. Charles
        humid gray sunshine
we were lovers again then
  bliss   smiles   and our comfortable silence
        you sang as we walked
        i wrote as we sat
both of us photographed this east coast jungle
        of concrete history – a mass of frisky people
you were my photographer then
        focused on me – fisheye
a bombastic frësch klesch everywhere
    devotee of the eccentric style
i was focused on my life fabric
at home in the City by the Bay
    on the dock – in the fog
 i remember your melancholy quiet –
i came home to see the sun breakthrough the fog
    feel the mist upon my face
        love the eccentric style again
   changing landscape of emotions
mourning my lost emblem

Rose City Blues # 10

endeavor to be worthy
                    of a pale blue heart
  a fine wine   red as a blush
          that grows in delight as it ages
a bombastic frësch klesch
          red in gentility
bred to age fine silver
          dictated wanderlust
          quelled dissention
to rest up here or push on thru?
     a light touch nurtures
                    a fixed design
three white stripes – Juve Gold
     frësch in every way
          perfectly endeavored to balance
     discreetly changing landscape
from the outside in   fantastic – bombastic
          frësch in every way

mixed energy

flowing landscape of colors
  cascade of vivid emotions
    light switch stability
        settles on black and white
  the non-colors of melancholy
    light switch insomnia
brilliant landscape changing
        every rainbow color shimmers
    joyful exuberance on me
  mixed states mixed messages
perception a filter colored by experience
 as changing mental landscapes
    focus stable blacks
  as dynamic floating clouds
    rain brilliant colors on me
 white as a pulsar exploding
        orgasmic pleasure for all

Burnside Bridge

unsteady energy   angry
        pace forlorn on sad eyes
    a visceral experience
        bloody knuckles on stone
    woken from spiraling chaos
  a beige clean white smoke
        layers follow diffusion
    in the calm cascade of understanding

unified theory

thence nothing whatsoever
lest we find ourselves alone
head gone mad from the subtle erotic explosions
how often is it that we fall?
after so long in perfect strides
perchance her wanton ado
left perilous melancholy
oh hadst our goblet glee
never damn your haste to love
for where is a gift lost before bestowed –
that beautiful bounty which comforts pleasure and leaves
us feeling whole
a penchant for the divine   walking verbose –
we never tire of being close
how often can one call her amor`
has no clever been lost like this before
i want   for there is no-thing
beyond desiring a bum – lost in Dharma
can our dignity claim respite from within
no fewer than before – we talk to lose our sight –
fancied match a delight
in taste we wash our throes in passionate flowers
for it is she you love in all this haste or
was it she who claimed the head of the lion
and left me wanting evermore inclined

No-thing

walk, talk no-thing
sang words of azure
no-thing new words
zen joy streaming vibes in search of
strong women like disco lemonade
strong women like disco lemonade
good-luck she said,
puzzled by vagary
azure is joy!
whom am i?
the bearer of sunshine
good-luck she said,
as the two ambled on
good-luck is the order of no-thing
just like kids playing tag
no-thing
beyond the vigilante art
you could be it!
its no-thing
no-thing
chasing liquid sand of molten colors
on ethereal streams –
photographing concrete dreams
its no-thing
azure is joy!
i am sunshine!

Visceral Experience

cascade strokes like clockwork on crushed chips
        knuckled and swollen like a force on concrete
    momentum wins during psychosis
        snapped clean and frësch
down drops the veil of bitter hate
    the least forgotten of all thy shapes
        circles swimming in squares
        feigning whimsical smiles
empty space reads like vignettes
    whitewashed on every eye i see with
        brushed copper in a pickled sky
    loosely wrangled white clouds
falling on self-thoughts about tomorrow
    would it suffice to leave a lover behind
like spent cigarette butts in sculpted glass ash-trays
                on wet tables – in dive bars
        with half-full pint glasses
    hussies in pain playing for the divine
a dream-like balm to cover ashes
    burnt from winking narcotics
        smoked and drunk on wet tables in dive bars after
three a.m.
        chasing manic screams
crushed thin by momentum

verbose zen

i find mornings to be vindictive
opposite expectations
waking to thoughts of you asleep
somewhere-else eyes closed in a semi-dream
stating pictures of how you left
vivid words as to how i feel
scrawled on wishes
as i remember them – hands grinning
you skipped in front of me
then vanished
replaced with mornings, vindictive
morose in its wake less irony
no ions pippin` energy
passing the root in time
swimming in a sea of memories
and kicking hard for the surface
to find a spiraling mind in my upward design
for soon the morning comes again
with its vindictive soul leaving me a smile
like zen words of meek and prey
who shall inherit mornings with vindictive souls-
after long waking nights in a bar
smoking smooth cool joy like butter
pray as we often will
on hip nights in jersey weather
we drink carousing blue cheese women
like ice cream on a hot day melting sloppy

drops like the rebel rousing doctrine
  eyeing the shell to eat the soul
    of blue cheese women who taste better
in the cool of morning sun after a night of explorative fun -
while shimmers glitter on peripheral hijinks
a premature anger unleashed
serving signs – egalitarian literalist bum
Dharma dogs speaking sanguine tongues
  chrome – silver reflections of highlights in gold
the white paint on concrete which guides our lives
is burned away   lingering interstitially
we escape the direction
    etching our names on cave walls
meditate with the Tao like the child says
    be the carved block which is uncarved
at the moment of entropic joy
i am a mitigated whore
    Didactic melancholy hedged against holy smiles
the supreme attitude relinquishes all power reluctantly a
morning star brigade relents no-thing
    upon blonde fields of black clad stars
tattooed on the apex of the trail to the labia
soft-oranje‘ lightning along golden lines
    outlining curves to loose a rational mind in
releasing creative chaos to hone one’s spiritual vision

zoom!

midnight in the Rose City
manic streams like hallucinogenic dreams
        zoom zoom zoom
standing in the vellum
photographing the streets as long black skirts
swaying in the night
    hand plucked wild flowers to me
green stems – purple marigolds   ‘here you go’
midnight joy is streaming by
zoom zoom zoom

311 News

play me like a fiddle she said
your touch is like a finely tuned harmonica
sung by a drunken Dylan lucid on acid
with Romeo crying in the back -
his Juliet is off frolicking with women
play with me - on me - touch me, stroke me - want me
more! you feel so good she said
pacing my orgasms to a bakers dozen + one
with her knees pinned to her chest
breasts bare - nipples arrested
as i enter the wet gash between her thighs
this greedy orgasm whore when favored on-top
Juliet laughs as she prances by a prone Don Giovanni
maybe i am lucid on acid
for Romeo follows me everyday
crying that his love has slain the velvet heart

mania junkie

no, it could not happen like such a whore would
        without money and a little friendship for dinner
the phone beeps   and on comes death
                    of a former lover
five more kisses and a quickie on the bed
                    legs pinned in an Indian style
                    position against her breasts
            lips shaved and soft as a deepened
            response enters her
together we cum then off i go – finding the phone call
as surreal as not believing i am an escort without pay
or a friend on a booty call
            as i am one who doesn't believe
in a meth whores transparency or clarity of words
                    between unwritten motives
                    contrasting scarlet shades
        when no color yields emotion
        without shades in the grayscale
hues like burnt oranje`
blue skies of carling colors strewn on languid canvas
        latched to fold-away doors
            riding in a dump truck down I-5
another master is wandering in the Himalayas
strewn on perception altered
            by the ether of high altitude

El Frësco Klesch

eighteen since i remember black days
        with sunny nights so long in a stupor
chasing realities doors at once surreal never sublime
        lyrical words wrapped on a light pole
some def jams are better left unsaid
but not this little ditty
   an urban punk myth for a hipster rose city
        the future mayor – frësch on the corner
     like a pimps black jacket – three white stripes
famed fourth grandfather of Hip Hop
        three transcendental black men
one crazy cracker -spinning mad philosophical rhymes
of chemistry and quantum futures
    surreal jams of def lyrical words
        frësch in every way –
black days for sunny nights

light switch physiology

as is – it goes far beyond a simple light switch
tears impact further chaos screams
from infinitesimal cosmos of disinfectant thoughts

as is – i go forward stumbling-staggering
i find my head on the floor
cold rocks and cobblestone
in the north park blocks wind whips blossoms
like a snow storm blanketing canvas
it's snowing said a jogger in red unlike Azure

as is – my life regrets the comfort of golden pillows
lost in white seas laced with vivid memories
painted lovingly on a canvas of pale skin

as is – no communication walks beyond Thursdays at three
- with silence a storm in my memory
as tears further white pillows

us blues

trickle down frolicking in a darkened pub
  with whiskey flowing shots like only once before
welcome to a post-911 world of scared lovers`
propagating terrorist lifestyles
while driving weapons of mass destruction
  on suburban asphalt fields where hate grows without water or soil
hidden behind blinds that keep out the light
of once beautiful blue sky days
  another casualty of fossil fuel combustion
a side effect of overzealous breeding
a kid like remnant of our fundamentalist farming ideal
  with parents of the day who feed their kids
spiteful bits of hate like its sugar-coated candy filled with joy

deconstructing l+j+k

on the night after a mourning star gelled rose
  it was like an air raid siren telling me you were there

no pity after a 2-nil loss to some white-capped fools
    with Jonny the fish in tow
two ambling impaired lads
chant their way in fine voice onto posh b-day parties
in elegant Japanese galleries

days beyond knowing how hate lingered in a heart
      where the words i love you once whispered from
pale lips
  your palm on my arm scenting memories
laced with phototropic cigarettes
      a hug that lasts two days
intensity for two minutes – holding each other as the
ocean caresses the shore
   scents and sensations i wondered if i needed
      but what makes it left of right when you leave me in
line?

no-thing dictates resolve in the zen words of manic motions
days beyond first contact when no memory of orchestration exists
i cannot see a path to fathom
or the reasons to believe humanity can be trusted
with a greater good beyond selfish me

a fortnight beyond seeing you again
i cannot deny how drastic altering failures
lie on me as this psychosis listens
very unlike vibes in you – in your haste & waste
the unity in god relates to chaotic energy intertwined
each to the divine

kat calls

soft pale sky blue in spring
    precursor to a dark sultry summer
sky – filled yellow sunshine shears
    breeze flows free like drapery in Paris
        our romance smiles for history to watch
on the street, in the square
bodies call each other heavenly design
    a temple of careful joy tended for a sublime guru
    perched on bull rock remembering Joshua Tree

Ashbury Dreams

Ashbury dreams like the tingle along the spine
          in a late fall foggy sunday
                    in a city by the bay

Ashbury dreams like walking cold under light sheets
          where fog rolls in at four-o'clock
mist falls by eight and the Golden Gate is socked in

Ashbury dreams like curb junkies
          in a city by the bay filled with neo-hippies
in open-air markets on wharf-lined streets
          where sea lions play like children

Ashbury dreams like barefoot woman
          clad in colored skirts
beggars of bohemia playing the harmonica
          as fog corners the city late Sunday

Ashbury dreams like kissing
                    on the dock late in the evening with
                    histories romance
          playing a love tune in the city by the bay

laurel thirsts First Fridays

demons come when love exits an unlit stage
on versatile days when the sun begins to sag
and evenings fade brilliant sound tapestries
draped over tiled brick contrasting age
and a once known history
of butterfly paintings painted on skin
like the Technicolor brick of storied kisses
in cabs late into the night
stories like the history
of star-crossed pursuit players
tabled in the corner booth surrounded
by compatriots of the proletariat slackers
laughter is the love of beer and drunkenness
the same laced red walls
are in shadow from directed spotlights
on a table where lovers first flirted with touch
laughter and fire mix well
on days when the sun starts to sag
and both clearly see blue skies
and cloud hopping skirts
flowered like color joy - dripping from fingers
supple with the pulse of comfort
like remembering Azure double-capped
by fresh pints of water

                    finished with laughter at loveable friends
          accepting of the story   as they
witness it transcend zen joy in grayscale colors
                    Technicolor brilliance is love replaced
                    with demons laughing
          at the comfort of skirts
regrettable but not forgotten
          until the purge revolts
and   i   i find myself sitting
in that corner booth one year later
          alone   with a smile and lit fag
     remembering the joy of the story as it unfolds

Rose City Blues # 13

something at last to say
long before your words echo a silent film
maybe it is how we find autumn a period of quiet triumph
or it's the time of sagging afternoon sun
with warm evenings that turn to cool nights
wanderlust walks stark streets
in a restless Rose City
the evening warmer than the day
and no full moon to be found
soon the Jordanian finds me on the street
with a Russian stripper in tow
and cigarettes that smoke loudly
as her deep accent
reflects the sexual movements of her body
so in-tuned to evoking a physical response in patrons
with dark supple skin
her perky erect breasts poking outward
from a skin tight black shirt upon sleek black pants
in her dark euroslut style she eyes El Mack`
standing clad with lit fag
trailing smoke rings by the lion's mystery
a sly smile streaks His face
as the Russian stripper reaches for a cig

she insinuates her body next to his
the buzz of industry hums
like the silence of spiteful lovers
and unlike the hiss of electricity
racing through the power lines on the street
like horny lovers racing in foreplay
long in anticipation of the tactile rage of sex to cum
for Russian strippers, the Jordanian and El` Mack
forty-one waits to hail triumph
for the answer is forty-two
yet what is that really   but   a little no-thing
of smiles + infinity
where no-thing rests on transparent honesty
in truth of lies
opens a buzz latent with smiles
from a tactile industry
a hard blues note
in a manic rose city

say – hey!

say you   hey   why?
i walked alone beyond
streets blind by silent life
devoid to reality of the crystal effect
languishing armor of ill-equipped
hues to match the furor of you
hey   why?
say   no   hey   maybe?
we can chat again soon
on this corner of crusted lucid pills
a touch of the whispery benign dreams
affected by sharp hues
in addled minds consumed
by a quiet chaos - lost to drug addled hysteria
where vivid Technicolor words
reflect the furor of you
say!   hey you?
kiss me once more on this corner -
please?

ex-pat news

where am i moving towards?
    a star split in long strides
forgetting all the future as a memory
        where do i hide?
    as the moon seeks to light a path
to walk with eyes that cannot see
        steps to place on paved markers
of zealous over consumption
what is the moniker?
    of mornings gelled by fascist fanatics
        leading the weak to fear
while the patriots drink cool mountain streams
        in a thousand pints of beer
                consumed from a bar stool

Rose City Blues # 3

mania runs like a swift wind
as the temperature changes
drastic endeavors lead to
morning stars of vivid screams
along Technicolor skin
invincible as much as i am invisible
from regret and longing
the silent loneliness forges
the conscious streams forward
moving forward perpetual
when darkness falls on blind eyes groping a wall
the man sitting still in a silent sea
of people - no one knows
i am still silent

59 cents

sonic dreams
of sensei-screams
in rapture alone a star
mourning a triumph
i cannot share with you
early morning dreams
like waking rapid eyes
flutter to the tune
of fifty - nine cents for a dollar

underworld

below freezing temperatures pursue the best night photog-
raphy
something in the crisp air dynamics
gives even-light and brilliant shadow detail
captured by only the craziest of seeing eyes
long lonely nights with your thought dreams
the failure characters who threaten and entertain your
nightly existence
isn't it like the rose city to house such a manic view
of tall spire radio wave towers under a park ele-
phant stone green
orange-yellow cast from sodium light
and the neon lines of a phantom design

Audible Reality

strange is the sound of silent explosions
like girls yelling greetings from the street below
where no one faintly moves with the rustle
of latent Fall color
dripping from ironic lunacy as i
stand on the balcony staring at no one
a smirk of audible Hallucinations
replacing the fog of creating collage of mania junkies
who dominate the field of vision
of the world i create in
out there where my hallucinations in audible form
are a reality to someone who knows what i am
\- sees what i do
let her love burst with joy like the message she
placed in the silence of my creating mind

Brugh Azul

night in the city comes swift
    for those who know long waking nights
when exhaustion only ends the lucid pace
    to wild-eyed thoughts chasing each other like colorful tracers
where being in love is like a three-dimensional helix of two separate strands
    which left to their own devices
will find their 3-D structure a self-binding chaotic mess
like the difference in crystalline water
    entropy comes for all of us
some just accelerate faster towards the third law of thermodynamics

night in the city leads to early morning rambling
illuminated by a neon blue green light
  the air is saturated with manic visions
        like a supernatural glow stick carried by the poor as flagsticks
to light the destructive path of the rich

how eerie?
it is to view a manic rose city from the dark
wet tiles of asphalt laid continuously
cover land where rain used to dissipate
the white lines in rows
numbered one to thirty-five
here where graffiti from kids is childish art of
modern culture
aggrandizing the selfish view of self at the center
where all good souls never stay long
due to crowded orbits like a gypsy
water roams chaotic futures of my good heart
lost in the gutter which flooded the streets
next to a parking lot on Flanders
where blue mail-trucks once parked perfectly
a-lined on dirt

untitled muse

the cold comes like a December with sunshine
as the pavement sits wet from early morning rainout
  its enough for now to sit here
        dreaming of the many ways
liquid moves as i sip warm café
        waiting for the muse to dance and twirl by
like curly pig-tailed hippy chicks beyond repose
    whose smiles glitter with starlet gold

Rose City Blues # 8

9:28 am, Che` just exited on a schwinn 10-speed
after late hours at the café`
        cigarettes smoke themselves to oblivion
    the politics of druggies and sex fiends lay on the ground
like blank faces on passerbys
        who live unknown stories of woe and joy
we should have forgotten some of the words we shared
  for they left the lingering images of meth addled
mug shots
        welcome to mania without the intelligence

10:30 am, can i sleep driven to fill the discrete
moments of time in a day
    like a studio wall parsed with yellow
circa sections of nudes and surreal urban nights
  in a manic state filtered by waves of mota
 lingering like vapors of burned cigarettes
    as my conscious mind gathers from a cattle prod
i await this tidal explosion of crystal understanding
    a liquid taste of unending melancholy
       drips from lips red in blue holes
lost to the ought-four beers i drank in whiskey nights
        of mania blues - where i alter my spirits
to raise my glass

Mania Blues # 2

wrinkles upon wrinkles in a gray-fold matter
around the same answer again
one layers up i spin reaching apex holds
this life they say is just misfiring synapses and chemical imbalances
some chemicals i know well - some i do not
the imbalance is idiosyncratic or artistic,
manageable and ballistic
apex to valley and back again
is a way to be aware of a life raging through us
apex to valley and off i go again
to skip cobbled streets in a manic rose city
as happy as i am - this city, celebrates
its weird wired clique
of modern social castes
phobic and stark by day – eerily vibrant at night
with contrasting characters of daylight wanderlust
that leads them to the contrast of shadow in night
exposure to a lit energy missing from caste` life

in days where social lepers taint the air blue
for the early onset of mania blues

Azure's Words

who forseeth our love
i foreswear to measure myself drunk
woe or melancholy vehemence
success hast a perilous neverland
say thee all for a whimsical chance
forgotten or forgone along some dirty road
where hookers sleep with the rich
i will wash the feet
of the next man whose name is Azure
for only he in his Quaker clothes leads me
to remembrance of the words He wrote
only their similarity to the hallucinogenic words
dancing in my head
Azure is the same crazy as me

ljk's muse

i keep looking for romantic residuals outside the drink
      migraines are a cost to forget
                  how non-linear life really is
my camera eye does not fail to remind me
          that humility is a gift i may regret
          as your choice of a gin and tonic at the tube
pale neon blue leaves more lines for my pen
     what next is said forgets not
          with my beer i like a shot of whiskey
     to place my black pen to white paper
          and place my photographs to words in Technicolor
                filtered through zones in black and white
          at a bar, like the Annex
in a dark red basement
                where my nudes once debuted
i lit my cigarettes
          always refusing to ask my words to spiral
   my crazy quiet with bursting interludes
idle chatter   spoken in a clear cadence
          i wrote mania blues there
my sympathetic rose city outside waiting to send down my next design
          i am here with a cigarette and coke
                  waiting for the muse to dance by

Daft Hands

be soft like my hand
    as i stretch upon you only seconds
one remembers the first time
        or the first with someone you like

    for the romantics   no-thing

    for the rational   loop-holes

    for the existential   freedom

hussies love to fuck a daft prick!

jive cup

clink – clink drops the coins into a paper cup
for street bums today
are the employed looking for something else
when times change they do the hard line
man drops out and find ok faces in a viewfinder
kodachrome is nothing on the silver emotion of
black and white - let the trends follow the wind
and soon we shall see how chaos dominates so
life is a checkerboard of random entropy
we expend all our energy to organize
neat square pegs for round holes
one size for us all as new trends lead to old hat
again the wind blows the next form of distraction
that is good for the waste it propagates

walking with royalty

as a kid, i was not privy to being a menace
until i could reason
though that came at age ten
my decision to be contrary to modern norms
came in 1993 with Sartre`, Emily, and Dylan
Jean-Paul Sartre` said our inability to deal with
the reality of existence
is existential strife
Emily Dickinson gave me my melancholy words
and showed me the nobility of crazy
Dylan Thomas gave me my words also, and the
propensity for drink, mania and women
like later, when i met Bukowski in the desert
impersonating an Irishman
drunk walkin as the crow flies
trying not to fall on rattlesnakes
the coyote tracking me as i weaved home
so i fled the desert la-la land for a manic rose city
and the coyote laughs as he tracks me

303 NW Park

bronze tan hue pads on marbled wood floors
    outside is the park where we met long ago
the faded wooden bench in the North Park Blocks
        sits by three fabled iron loops on the ground
i sit long enough to imagine a future
and past occurrence here
  the future - with the clarity of a young girl of two years
standing inside on marbled wood floors smiling at
someone in the park
  the past – was me on the park bench
                late at night in the cold dark
sitting just long enough to be
                        a silhouette for the camera
        it feels somewhat frësch in the rose city
    i sit on that bench with the sun on my face
        staring at the façade of rusted tan bronze hue

pole - to - pole

my timing in matters of love
        is off step by varying beats
my timing in sex is multiplied for her
                                and tantric for me
        as is the case for all mania junkies
   why ask who is born of a year and then some
        i was told it snowed in 1975 +1
  even so - why a manic rose city?
   on streets pounded with the cadence of latent loss
        only opposite polarities are truly separate
180-degrees out of phase
    we seek a divinity in wholeness
only to experience continual progress from
                pole - to - pole

Rose City Blues # 4

life is like many metaphors
    combined as one would place
    several vases on a window sill
        for flowers sit in the sun
so they wilt slowly from the loss of nutrients
    sustaining like humanity and a laundry list
hierarchical needs met via metaphors of growth
stagnation is Gods metaphor for the unexpected
        like finding mania junkies skipping in the park
or the knickers of the whore
        i brought home from the bar last night

Yamhill Pub Rant

fuckin` kids are everywhere who follow
   an act of themselves in love
like a playdate for a white collar on a Friday night
for fucks sake
          it's a punk bar!
go across the street or get a room with water martini's
   and coke lines so you can fuck
                              and your girl will want it
      this place just isn't romantic ya` wanker
i am such a daft prick
          a punk in my PBR and British army uni
you fucks - you're so polite it makes me sick
   black eyed Irish lads drinking for the women
   to hear their accent
          it wets them every time
fuckin` shite scousers from the north
          London fags in the south
   i hate them all for their dour airiness
the lovers and polite ones are soon replaced
          with black fags in white Irish suits
     they are black eyed IRA operatives
drinking beer in this pub
                    punk and drunk like goons

i am a daft prick for the things i say
but i do not live this life of falsities for myself
i am the original punk
like Buddha & Christ
i can sing slang   write poetry
or smoke a cigarette like a chemist
anarchy is a way to die if ever i wanted out of this
whores are what we all seek - spread legs are an accommodation
yet love is not something we share she said
on a cell phone as she came in the front door
you have to be cold in that tee-shirt
dancing with your green scarf like a dog in heat
nothing like the dark vamp who entered after her
a precursor to the four horseman
or is it a thousand voices calling
for the liberation of Palestine
Rosh shalom say the Zionists
a golden crown for those who are untouched
by long winded ramblings from this daft prick
the Yamhill Pub is a punk bar for fucks sake
they celebrate mania junkies here
so piss off and go home

Songs from 107

SEA – double TLE
Seattle spells shit to me
With a knick knack patty whack
Give the dog a bone
Why doesn't Seattle
Fuck off Home!

oh rose city, oh rose city
oh rose city is wonderful
we have tits ass and the Timbers
oh rose city is wonderful
tell me, can you hear seattle sing?
oh no! oh no! can you hear seattle sing?
oh no! oh no! can you hear seattle sing?
i don't hear a fucking thing
oh no! oh no! oh no!
oh rose city. oh rose city
oh rose city is wonderful
we have tits ass and the Timbers
oh rose city is wonderful

SEA – double TLE
Seattle spells shit to me
With a knick knack patty whack
Give the dog a bone
Why doesn't Seattle
Fuck off Home!

rant and chants
lads singing loud
beers flowing down

we're the greatest fucking lads
                    when we win
                    when we win
we're the greatest fucking lads
                    when we win
we're a rotten lot of bastards
                    when we lose
                    when we lose
we're a rotten lot of bastards
                    when we lose

tell me, can you hear seattle sing?
oh no! oh no!
can you hear seattle sing?
      oh no! oh no! can you hear seattle sing?
   i don't hear a fucking thing
      oh no! oh no! oh no!
oh rose city. oh rose city
      oh rose city is wonderful
we have tits ass and the Timbers
      oh rose city is wonderful

i was born in the rose city
      i will be true to my lads
   rose city till i die
   rose city till i die
i know i am – i'm sure i am
   rose city till i die
oh rose city. oh rose city
      oh rose city is wonderful
we have tits ass and the Timbers
      oh rose city is wonderful

i was born in the rose city
i will be true to my lads
rose city till i die
rose city till i die
i know i am – i'm sure i am
rose city till i die
tell me, can you hear seattle sing
oh no! oh no!
can you hear seattle sing?
oh no! oh no! can you hear seattle sing?
i don't hear a fucking thing
oh no! oh no! oh no!
oh rose city. oh rose city
oh rose city is wonderful
we have tits ass and the Timbers
oh rose city is wonderful

SEA – double TLE
Seattle spells shit to me
With a knick knack patty whack
Give the dog a bone
Why doesn't Seattle
Fuck off Home!
Say, where ever we may be
We are the famous Rose City
Cause we don't give a Fuck
and we don't give a shit
We're going to win the league Championship
Say, where ever we may be
We are the famous Rose City
Cause we don't give a Fuck
and we don't give a shit
We're going to win the league Championship

www.ingramcontent.com/pod-product-compliance
Lightning Source LLC
Chambersburg PA
CBHW030437120726
47903CB00003B/1008

* 9 7 8 0 9 7 6 8 5 6 0 0 9 *